I Jump

Claire Llewellyn
Illustrated by Garry Davies

RIGBY

I like to jump.
Do you like to jump?

No, I like to fly.

5

Do you like to jump?

No, I like to swim.

Do you like to jump?

No, I like to walk.

Do you like to jump?

Yes, I like to jump.

We like to
jump, jump, jump!